Awesome African Animals!

A+
books

Zebras Are Awesome!

by Megan Cooley Peterson

Consultant: Jackie Gai, DVM
Captive Wildlife Veterinarian

CAPSTONE PRESS
a capstone imprint

A+ Books are published by Capstone Press,
1710 Roe Crest Drive, North Mankato, Minnesota 56003
www.capstonepub.com

Library of Congress Cataloging-in-Publication Data
Peterson, Megan Cooley, author.
  Zebras are awesome! / by Megan Cooley Peterson.
    pages cm. — (A+ books. Awesome African animals)
  Summary: "Describes characteristics, habitat, behavior, life cycle, and threats to zebras living in the wild of Africa"—Provided by publisher.
  Audience: Ages 5–8.
  Audience: K to grade 3.
  Includes bibliographical references and index.
  ISBN 978-1-4914-1764-5 (library binding)
  ISBN 978-1-4914-1770-6 (paperback)
  ISBN 978-1-4914-1776-8 (eBook PDF)
1. Zebras—Juvenile literature. 2. Animals—Africa—Juvenile literature. I. Title.

  QL737.U62P48 2015
  599.665'7—dc23   2014023673

Editorial Credits

Erika Shores and Mari Bolte, editors; Cynthia Della-Rovere, designer;
Svetlana Zhurkin, media researcher; Morgan Walters, production specialist

Photo Credits

Getty Images: Buena Vista Images, 4—5; Minden Pictures: FLPA/Terry Andrewatha, 25; Newscom: ZUMA Press/Andy Rouse, 23 (middle); Shutterstock: Alexandra Giese, 12—13, Andrzej Kubik, 15 (top), Black Sheep Media (grass), throughout, Chantal de Bruijne, 7, Dmitri Gomon, 8, EcoPrint, 9 (bottom), 26, Eric Isselee, cover (top left, bottom), 11, 32, Francois van Heerden, 18, Harald Toepfer, 21, Hedrus, 16, Joe McDonald, 23 (top), Justin Black, back cover, 24 (top), Karel Gallas, 27, lumen-digital, 9 (top), Muskoka Stock Photos, 19, Pal Teravagimov, 6, sharps, 22—23, Simon_g, cover (top right), 1, 29, Stacey Ann Alberts, 14—15, Stefanie van der Vinden, 17, Steve Allen, 20, Stuart G. Porter, 28—29, SurangaSL (zebra stripes background), back cover and throughout, Villiers Steyn, 10, 24 (bottom)

Note to Parents, Teachers, and Librarians

This Awesome African Animals book uses full color photographs and a nonfiction format to introduce the concept of zebras. *Zebras are Awesome!* is designed to be read aloud to a pre-reader or to be read independently by an early reader. Photographs help listeners and early readers understand the text and concepts discussed. The book encourages further learning by including the following sections: Table of Contents, Glossary, Read More, Internet Sites, and Index. Early readers may need assistance using these features.

Printed in China by Nordica.
0914/CA21401520
092014   008470NORDS15

Table of Contents

Striking Stripes 4

Life on the Grasslands 12

Growing Up Zebra 24

Saving Zebras 28

Glossary 30

Read More 31

Internet Sites 31

Critical Thinking Using the Common Core . 31

Index 32

Striking Stripes

A hungry lion slinks through Africa's tall grasses. The lion is on the hunt. It spots a group of zebras. The black-and-white stripes of the zebras' coats blend together. The lion can't pick out a single zebra to chase. It moves on to find easier prey. The zebras stay safe.

Zebras are mammals famous for their dazzling stripes. Many African animals have brown coloring to blend in with their surroundings. But zebras hide in plain sight. Scientists believe the zebras' stripes break up the outlines of their bodies. Lions, hyenas, and cheetahs have trouble telling where one zebra ends and another begins.

There are three kinds of zebras. Each kind has a different stripe pattern. Grevy's zebras have thin, close stripes. Some plains zebras have light brown "shadow" stripes between black stripes. Wide stripes cover a mountain zebra's back. All zebras have black skin under their coats.

Grevy's zebra

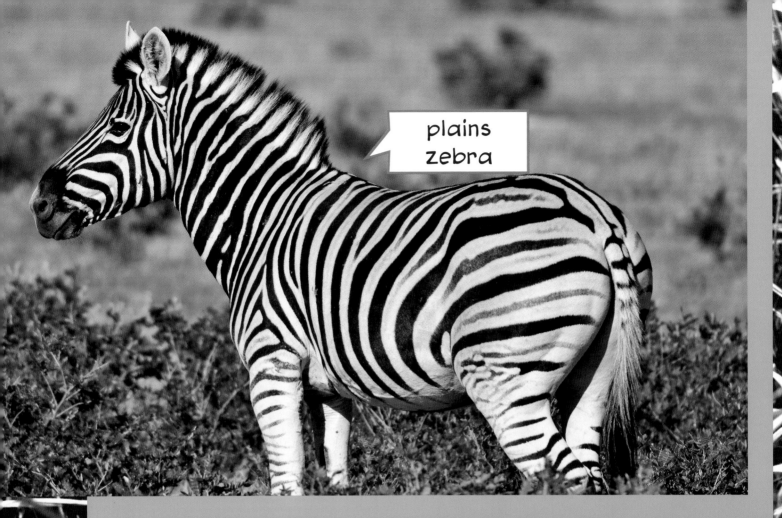

plains zebra

mountain zebra

9

Zebras are related to horses and donkeys. Zebras weigh up to 900 pounds (408 kilograms). They stand up to 5 feet (1.5 meters) tall at the shoulders.

Like horses, zebras have large ears and eyes. A zebra's ears move to hear sounds. Zebras also have excellent vision. At night a zebra can see as well as an owl!

Life on the Grasslands

All wild zebras live in Africa. Grevy's zebras are found in Kenya and Ethiopia. They live on dry grasslands. Plains zebras roam the savannas and grasslands of eastern and southern Africa. Mountain zebras are found in small areas of Namibia and Angola.

Africa

Where Zebras Live

13

Zebras live in groups called herds.
When in danger, the herd flees together.
Sometimes zebras join herds of giraffes and
wildebeests to stay safe.

Zebras work together to keep the herd safe. At night one zebra stays awake to watch for danger so the rest of the herd can sleep. Talk about teamwork!

Can you imagine eating for up to 19 hours a day? Zebras do! They munch mostly on grass. They also eat bark, leaves, and roots.

The food zebras eat doesn't contain many nutrients. Zebras have to eat a lot to get the energy they need.

A zebra's teeth never stop growing.
Luckily, all that grazing wears down their teeth.

A zebra's teeth also come in handy for scratching and biting. A pair of zebras will stand tail to nose and nibble each other. They also swish away flies with a flick of their tails.

Zebras never travel far from watering holes. They use their hooves to dig for water in dry streambeds.

While drinking, zebras stay on the lookout for predators. Zebras usually drink in the morning when lions are resting.

Zebras use their legs and hooves to stay safe. When in danger, zebras will run away if they can. They can run up to 40 miles (65 kilometers) per hour.

Zebras kick enemies with their sharp hooves. A single kick from a zebra's back leg can break a lion's jaw.

Growing Up Zebra

Small family groups make up a zebra herd. Each group has one stallion, or male zebra. Each family also includes a few mares and their young, called foals.

Mares give birth to a single foal. Newborn foals weigh between 70 and 80 pounds (32 and 36 kg). They have fuzzy coats.

Foals can walk 20 minutes after birth. Within an hour they trot along with their mothers. A foal knows its mother by her smell and stripes. Each zebra has its own unique stripe pattern.

Foals stay close to their mothers for two or three years. In the wild, zebras can live up to 25 years.

Saving Zebras

Some of the land where zebras live has been turned into farms. Zebras are also hunted. Loss of land and hunting has left mountain and Grevy's zebras endangered.

Today people work to save zebras. They protect the land where zebras live. Scientists also study zebras to learn how to help these awesome African animals.

Glossary

endangered (in-DAYN-juhrd)—in danger of dying out

foal (FOHL)—a zebra that is less than one year old

grassland (GRASS-land)—a large, open area without trees where grass and low plants grow

herd (HURD)—a large group of animals that lives or moves together

hoof (HOOF)—the hard covering on an animal's foot

mammal (MAM-uhl)—a warm–blooded animal that breathes air; mammals have hair or fur; female mammals produce milk to feed their young

mare (MAIR)—an adult female zebra

nutrient (NOO-tree-uhnt)—parts of food, like vitamins, that are used for growth

predator (PRED-uh-tur)—an animal that hunts other animals for food

prey (PRAY)—an animal hunted by another animal for food

savanna (suh-VAN-uh)—a flat, grassy area of land with some trees

stallion (STAL-yuhn)—an adult male zebra

unique (yoo-NEEK)—only one of its kind

Read More

Reade, Clara. *Zebras*. Powerkids Readers: Safari Animals. New York: PowerKids Press, 2013.

Rustad, Martha E. H. *Zebras and Oxpeckers Work Together*. Animals Working Together. Mankato, Minn.: Capstone Press, 2011.

Zobel, Derek. *Zebras*. Blastoff! Readers. Animal Safari. Minneapolis: Bellwether Media, 2011.

Internet Sites

FactHound offers a safe, fun way to find Internet sites related to this book. All of the sites on FactHound have been researched by our staff.

Here's all you do:
Visit *www.facthound.com*
Type in this code: 9781491417645

 Super-cool stuff!

Check out projects, games and lots more at
www.capstonekids.com

Critical Thinking Using the Common Core

1. Describe how a zebra's striped coat protects it from predators. (Key Ideas and Details)

2. Look at the photos on pages 20-21. Explain why one zebra in both photos is not drinking. (Integration of Knowledge and Ideas)

3. How do zebras use teamwork? Why is teamwork important to zebras? (Key Ideas and Details)

Index

colors, 4, 6, 8, 26

foals, 24, 25, 26, 27

food, 16, 17

hearing, 11

herds, 14, 24

hooves, 20, 22, 23

kinds of
    Grevy's, 8, 12, 28
    mountain, 8, 12, 28
    plains, 8, 12

life span, 27

predators, 4, 21, 23

range, 12–13

relatives of, 10

sight, 11

size, 10, 24

speed, 22

teeth, 18, 19